The Royal Baby

COMMEMORATING THE BIRTH OF HRH PRINCE GEORGE

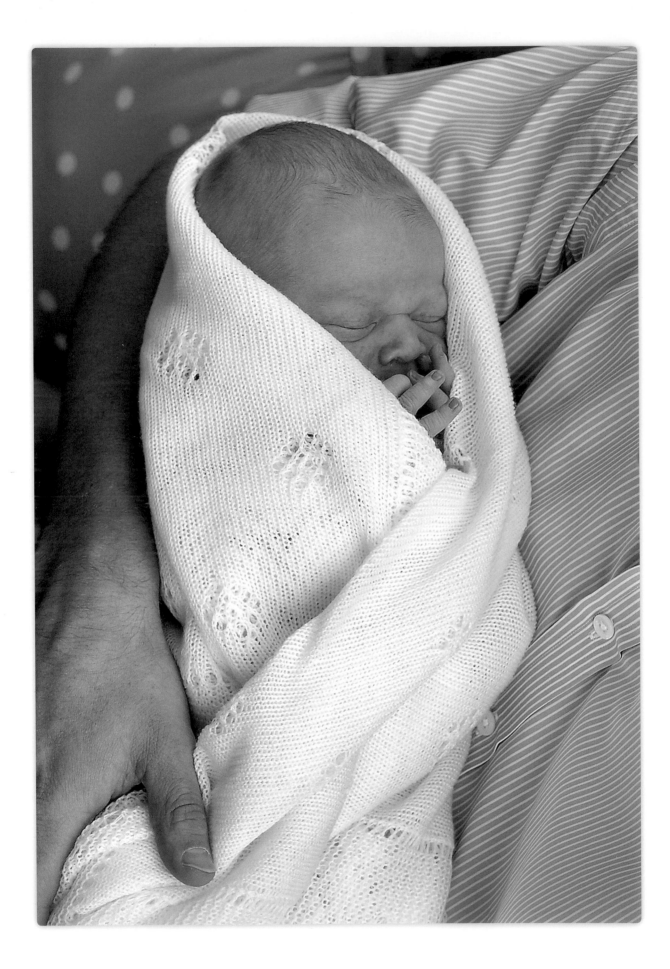

The Royal Baby

COMMEMORATING THE BIRTH OF HRH PRINCE GEORGE

ANNIE BULLEN

PITKIN
· GUIDES ·

Written by Annie Bullen.
The moral right of the author has been asserted.

Edited by Gill Knappett.
Picture research by Gill Knappett and Lindsey Smith.
Cover designed by Katie Beard.
Designed by Glad Stockdale.

All images by kind permission of Press Association Images,
except for the following:
Getty Images: Inside front cover, pp3, 12 left, 24 left, 26 top,
31 top left, 35 bottom, 44 right, 46 both, inside back cover;
Mary Evans Picture Library: pp4 top, 12, 13 both, 14, 15 top, 20,
30 (National Magazines Company) left, 35 top and centre, 48, 49
top, 51 top (Interfoto/ Sammlung Rauch), 53 top (Francis Frith),
53 bottom (Illustrated London News Ltd); The Middleton Family,
2011: p6 bottom left; Bridgeman Art Library: pp18 (Neil Holmes),
49 bottom (National Maritime Museum, London), 50, 51 bottom,
52 (The Royal Collection © 2011 HM Queen Elizabeth II),
54 (Sudeley Castle, Gloucestershire/ Mark Fiennes), 55 top (The
Royal Collection Trust), 55 bottom (Private Collection/ The
Stapleton Collection); TopFoto: pp21, 58 bottom; Royal Archives
(© 2013 HM Queen Elizabeth II): p34 centre; English Heritage:
p34 bottom; Rex Features: p37 top left; Royal Collection Trust
(© HM Queen Elizabeth II): p58 centre; Camera Press London:
p59 (John Swannell).

A CIP catalogue for this book is available from the British Library.
Published by Pitkin Publishing, The History Press, The Mill,
Brimscombe Port, Stroud, Gloucestershire GL5 2QG, UK
www.pitkin-guides.com

Printed in Canada.
ISBN 978-1-84165-461-4   1/13

PITKIN
·GUIDES·

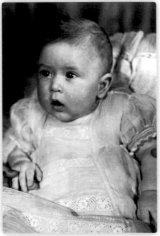

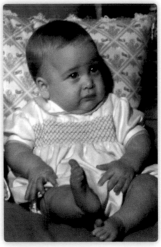

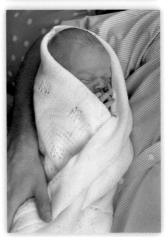

Top to bottom: Queen Elizabeth,
Prince Charles, Prince William and
Prince George as babies.

Contents

'Wonderful Baby, Beautiful Baby'

The miracle of new life swept away memories of a long and tiring labour. The couple, sitting closely together, wanted nothing more than to gaze at, touch and hold their baby boy. The three of them were now a family and this was a private time to be savoured. But the new parents, aware that this was no ordinary birth, knew that their peaceful interlude could not last. As the and their baby got to know each other, the pressure of public expectation outside the hospital room was growing by the minute.

While Kate and William, the Duchess and Duke of Cambridge, marvelled at the fierce rush of protective love that takes all new parents by surprise, the world waited, impatient for news of this baby, one day to be king, a child destined to live his whole life with the eyes of the public upon him.

On Monday 22 July 2013, the hottest day of the year, George Alexander Louis, the new Prince of Cambridge, was born in the air-conditioned private Lindo Wing of St Mary's Hospita

Right: A proud Prince Charles carries the newborn William as he and Princess Diana leave hospital for their home at Kensington Palace.

Right: Catherine Middleton, aged three.

Far right: Prince William, aged three.

Above: Proud parents Catherine and William introduce their new baby to the world as they leave St Mary's Hospital.

ldington at 4.24 in the afternoon, weighing 8lbs 6oz. His ents, knowing they would have little privacy once the th was made public, wanted to share those first precious urs alone with him. They managed to delay the long-aited announcement until 8.30 that evening, when the ion and the world rejoiced.

Breaking with royal tradition, an official notification the birth was given to the press by an email sent from nsington Palace. Only then was the framed foolscap letin, detailing the time of birth and the baby's weight, ivered to Buckingham Palace through the Privy rse door, before being fixed to an ornate gold-painted el by The Queen's communications secretary, Aisla nderson, helped by a liveried footman. The easel stood Buckingham Palace forecourt, just inside the railings. another nod to the modern age, Clarence House then eeted the details on Twitter.

The humid evening air outside Buckingham Palace ckled with excitement as a large and growing crowd essed forward to take photographs of the historic cument, signed by surgeon-gynaecologist Marcus tchel, who had delivered the new Prince. Even he was oved by the birth, murmuring 'wonderful baby, beautiful by' as he left the Lindo wing that evening.

Joy and genuine delight were expressed by tourists and Londoners, excited visitors and those who rushed to the palace as soon as they heard the news. A huge full moon rose above the building as the crowds heard that new father Prince William had said that he and Kate 'could not be happier'. His own father, Prince Charles, was 'enormously proud to be a first-time grandfather', while The Queen was 'delighted' to welcome her first great-grandson who will, one day, take his own place on the British throne.

The long-awaited news that Kate, accompanied by her husband, had checked into the exclusive private wing of St Mary's Hospital – where William was born 31 years earlier – turned that hot Monday in July into a day of fevered expectation for the British people. She and William, who stayed with her during the birth, had managed to give most of the hundreds of waiting journalists and photographers the slip, by using a side entrance when they arrived in the early hours of the morning.

The Prince Who Will Be King

Kate and William spent the first night after the birth in their private suite at St Mary's with their newborn son. The baby Prince slept peacefully, unaware of the weight of history, past and present, on his tiny shoulders. He will be the 43rd monarch since William the Conqueror won the English Crown at the Battle of Hastings in 1066 and he will eventually be the eighth monarch to descend from Queen Victoria.

Prince George, The Queen's third great-grandchild (but first great-grandson after Peter Phillip's girls, Savannah and Isla) will one day be Head of the Armed Forces, Supreme Governor of the Church of England, head of state of 16 countries and, possibly, if the role continues, Head of the Commonwealth, which spans 54 nations worldwide and embraces mor than two billion citizens.

Left: The happy family greet the waiting press and well-wishers with huge smiles, allowing the world a glimpse of the future king.

Far right: A tender moment: Kate transfers baby George from her arms to his proud father's. It was 'very emotional' and 'special' the Duchess said to press of the birth. 'Any parent must know what this feeling feels like.'

Prince George's birth means that for the first time since Queen Victoria's reign, when her great-grandson, the future Edward VIII, was born in 1894, the monarchy has three generations of heirs to the throne. In 1894 they were Queen Victoria's son Bertie, later Edward VII, his son, who became George V, and the ill-fated Edward VIII, who abdicated in 1936. Now the heirs are Prince Charles, heir presumptive Prince William and his son Prince George.

Left: Happy and relaxed, the new parents chat with the press about their young son. 'He's got her looks, thankfully,' laughed Prince William.

His birth was marked by two gun salutes, at Green Park
d the Tower of London, while the bells of Westminster
obey were rung in a celebratory peal lasting three hours
d technical wizardry turned the splashing water in the
afalgar Square fountains blue.

Of all the responses to the arrival of the latest addition
the Royal Family, perhaps the most heartfelt has been
at of his grandfather, The Prince of Wales. The Prince
who is close to both his sons, William and Harry,
aying an enormous part in their upbringing following
e tragic death of their mother, Princess Diana – was
early overwhelmed at the news. 'Both my wife and I are
erjoyed at the arrival of my first grandchild,' said the
ince, who was in Yorkshire with his wife, the Duchess
Cornwall. 'Grandparenthood is a unique moment in
yone's life, as countless kind people have told me in
cent months, so I am enormously proud and happy
be a grandfather for the first time,' he added.

The Prince of Wales, The Queen and the Duke of
Edinburgh, the baby's maternal grandparents Carole
and Michael Middleton, Prince Harry and other senior
members of the Royal Family were the first to be told
of Prince George's birth, before the public announcement
was made.

Royal history would have been
made if the baby had been a girl.
Under the new Succession to the
Crown Act, girls now have equal
succession rights as boys and
cannot be supplanted in the line of
succession by a younger brother.

Bringing Up a Future King

The Prime Minister, David Cameron, was sincere when he welcomed the 'wonderful moment for a warm and loving couple who have got a brand-new baby boy'.

The Duchess, in her early life as Kate Middleton, was brought up in a happy and caring family atmosphere by parents who worked hard to give her and her younger brother and sister the best childhood they could. Prince William's loving relationship with his mother, Princess Diana, was brought to an abrupt end when she died tragically in a motoring accident in Paris in 1997 when he was just 15 years old. But she had been a caring parent who loved her sons dearly, giving them the freedom and fun often denied to royal children in the past.

So young Prince George will have as normal an upbringing as possible, with two parents determined to let him enjoy as much privacy as they are able.

Although they will want his early life to be comparatively free from protocol and formality, they know they have to balance this desire with a respect for royal tradition. Their son, after all, will one day be head of state.

George will live with his parents at Apartment 1A at Kensington Palace where the 20 rooms, once belonging to William's great-aunt, Princess Margaret, have been refurbished. The large walled garden is an ideal private playground.

The young Prince and his mother and father may well spend much of their time at the Middleton's family home, a manor house with a tennis court, swimming pool and 18 acres in the quiet village of Bucklebury in Berkshire, the village where the young Kate grew up and

Right: Proud grandparents Carole and Michael Middleton were the first visitors to the private Lindo Wing to meet the young Prince, telling reporters as they left that baby George was 'absolutely beautiful'.

Far right: The Prince of Wales visits with wife Camilla, Duchess of Cornwall. 'I am enormously proud and happy to be a grandfather for the first time,' he told press earlier that day.

Above and below: Leaving hospital with George in his car seat, Prince William calmly carries out the task that can thwart many a new parent, securing his baby in the car.

spent her school holidays, away from Marlborough College. It is unlikely that George will be looked after by a full-time nanny at least for the first few months of his life, as Catherine will want him to experience the same family pleasures that she and her siblings enjoyed. New grandmother Carole Middleton may well be a key figure in George's early years, helping to look after her grandson as the Duchess returns to official duties.

The influence of his paternal grandparents will also be a strong one. Summer holidays at Balmoral, with all the outdoor pleasures that the Royal Family's Scottish estate affords, will be his, as will the traditional family Christmas at Sandringham, in Norfolk.

The royal custom of home schooling was firmly broken when Diana sent her young sons, William and Harry, first to nursery school, then to Wetherby pre-preparatory school before a time at Ludgrove School in Berkshire and thence to Eton College, a stone's throw from Windsor Castle.

Kate was educated at St Andrew's preparatory school in Berkshire, before boarding at Marlborough College. She and William met at St Andrews, Scotland's oldest university, when each studied there.

So it is likely that the young Prince of Cambridge will be educated away from home and the chances are that he will become an Eton student, following his father and Uncle Harry who both have fond memories of their schooldays at the Windsor college.

Below: Prince Charles lets his emotions show as he punches the air with joy on leaving the hospital.

A Royal Destiny

The year was 1921 and Britain was still recovering from the effects of the First World War. Young Prince Albert, the second son of King George V, shyly asked the pretty daughter of the Earl of Strathmore to be his wife. But the young woman, Lady Elizabeth Bowes-Lyon, turned him down.

'Bertie' was not to be deterred and asked her again the following year, when she was a bridesmaid to his sister, Princess Mary. But again he was disappointed. Despite his shyness, he did not give up. The following year his persistence paid off and the couple, the Duke and Duchess of York, were married in Westminster Abbey on 26 April 1923.

Bertie's father, the 'Sailor King' who had steered his people through the four years of wartime austerity, had changed the Royal Family's name in 1917 from Saxe-Coburg-Gotha to Windsor, showing his commitment to a fully British way of life.

George V had never expected to become king, but when his older brother, Prince Albert, died of influenza in 1892, his naval career was brought to an abrupt end. He assumed the duties of heir to the throne and married his brother's fiancée, Mary of Teck. They raised their family of five sons and a daughter at York Cottage on the Sandringham Estate in Norfolk. There was rejoicing on the arrival of their first child in 1894. The boy, whom they named Edward, was regarded by the nation as the future king and became heir presumptive when his grandfather, Edward VII, died in 1910 and his father ascended the throne.

Right: Prince George and Princess Mary (later King George V and Queen Mary) in 1906, with their children (from left): Princess Mary, Prince John (held by his mother), Prince Henry (seated at front), Prince George, Prince Edward (later King Edward VIII) and Prince Albert (later King George VI).

Far right: Lady Elizabeth Bowes-Lyon, aged seven, in 1907. She was to become Queen Elizabeth in 1937 and, later, the Queen Mother.

Right: Lady Elizabeth Bowes-Lyon with her family at Glamis Castle. Seated (from left): Lady Elizabeth Bowes-Lyon, Miss Betty Cator, Miss Betty Malcolm, Lady Strathmore, Lady Elphinstone, Lady Glamis. Sitting on the ground is Cecilia Bowes-Lyon, the daughter of Lord and Lady Glamis. Standing are: Lord Elphinstone, Lord Glamis, Lord Strathmore, Captain Malcolm and the Hon. James Stuart.

Although King George V was a second son and not born to rule, he had 18 years to prepare for kingship on the unexpected death of his elder brother in 1892. His own son, Prince Albert, Duke of York, was not so lucky. Dreading the public spotlight, and cherishing a peaceful and private home life, his world changed within a few days when his older brother, King Edward VIII, abdicated in December 1936, after ruling for only 11 months. Prince Albert, second in line to the throne, would become king.

Below: The newly married Duke and Duchess of York, Prince Albert and Lady Elizabeth Bowes-Lyon, at Bookham Station on their way to Polesden Lacey in Surrey at the start of their honeymoon. The couple, who married on 26 April 1923, were to become King George VI and Queen Elizabeth.

As Edward, Prince of Wales, grew to manhood his life became dissimilar to that of his younger brother, who, by the age of 28, was a happily married family man. Edward developed a reputation as a dilettante and a playboy – and he showed no signs of settling down. Bertie, who had served with both the Royal Navy and the newly formed Royal Air Force – becoming, in 1918, the first member of the Royal Family to qualify as a pilot – lived life very differently. After his marriage Bertie settled comfortably into life with his young wife at their home at 145 Piccadilly, undertaking royal duties with her, including a tour of Kenya and Uganda in 1924 and 1925. Although he suffered a lack of self-confidence and a dread of public speaking because of a persistent stammer, the support of his wife and services of a speech therapist, Lionel Logue, eased his anxiety. His wife, the former Lady Elizabeth Bowes-Lyon, the ninth of ten children of an energetic and loving family, helped him to enjoy life and to value a comfortable domestic situation.

And when, towards the end of 1925, they knew they were expecting their first child, due in the spring of 1926, their happiness was unbounded. They foresaw a close and happy family life, untroubled by heavy responsibility.

Princess Elizabeth

There was much joy in the Royal Family when, on 21 April 1926, a baby daughter was born to the Duke and Duchess of York in London. The news was of great interest to the British people, but there was no expectation that this baby would, one day, become queen, although she was third in the line of succession to the throne. There seemed no reason why her 'Uncle David', the Prince of Wales, the King's eldest son, should not succeed his father in due course.

Her parents, Elizabeth and Bertie, were living, temporarily, at 17 Bruton Street, Mayfair, a house which belonged to the grandfather of the Duchess who chose to have her baby at home. Princess Elizabeth was born, by Caesarean section, at 2.40am. Bulletins reassured the public that mother and baby were both doing well.

'We always wanted a child to make our happiness complete,' the Duke, delighted by the arrival of his daughter, wrote to his mother, Queen Mary. Her Majesty was clearly happy too, recording in her diary: 'Such a relief and joy,' adding that the new baby was 'a little darling with lovely complexion and pretty fair hair.'

Baby Elizabeth was not short of exquisite clothes, handmade from first-rate materials. The newspapers reported that her grandmothers, the Queen of England and Lady Strathmore, together with her mother, the Duchess of York, had personally stitched the Princess's layette, assisted by the inmates of charitable institutions, often 'poor gentlewomen', who helped to make the fine lawn and muslin frocks, and little bonnets and jackets.

The first grandchild of King George V was named Elizabeth Alexandra Mary – for her mother (Queen Elizabeth), the King's mother (Queen Alexandra), who had died six months earlier, and for her paternal grandmother (Queen Mary).

Right: Princess Elizabeth of York in her cradle.

Princess Elizabeth's upbringing, in a close-knit family
atmosphere, was very different from that of her father, whose
relationship with his own exacting father was often remote and
difficult. But the infant Elizabeth charmed her grandfather the
King, who doted on his beautiful baby granddaughter, paying
her the attention he had never given to his own children. She,
in turn, loved to chat and play with 'Grandpa England' and her
grandmother, Queen Mary.

Perhaps it was less of a surprise that she enjoyed her days
with her maternal grandparents – having raised ten children of
their own and with several grandchildren already, there was not
much that the Princess's mother's parents did not know about
entertaining young children.

Although the Duchess of York was as much a 'hands-on'
mother as her circumstances and duties permitted, the baby
Elizabeth had excellent care from her nanny, Clara Knight, known
as 'Alla', who looked after her young charge from the earliest days.

Above: The baby
Princess Elizabeth with
her mother, then the
Duchess of York.

Princess Elizabeth's christening ceremony, on 29 May, a few weeks after
her birth, was held in the private chapel at Buckingham Palace and
conducted by the Anglican Archbishop of York, Cosmo Gordon Lang,
who baptized her in the traditional Lily Font with water from the river
Jordan. Her godparents were King George V and Queen Mary (her paternal
grandparents), Claude Bowes-Lyon (her maternal grandfather), Prince
Arthur, Duke of Connaught (her father's great-uncle), Princess Mary
(her paternal aunt) and Lady Elphinstone (her maternal aunt).

Left: Princess Elizabeth
is christened at
Buckingham Palace.
Seated in the front
(left to right) are: Lady
Elphinstone (elder
sister to the Duchess
of York), Queen Mary,
the Duchess of York
with her daughter,
Princess Elizabeth, the
Countess of Strathmore
and Princess Mary
(sister of the Duke of
York). Standing (left
to right) are: the Duke
of Connaught, King
George V, the Duke of
York and the Earl of
Strathmore.

Right: Outside her home at 145 Piccadilly: two-year-old Princess Elizabeth with her nanny, Clara Knight.

The year following the birth of baby Elizabeth was a difficult one for her parents. The Duke and Duchess of York had been invited by the Australians to open the new Parliament House in Canberra. They would also promote trade between Britain and Australia, so the six-month tour was of economic as well as diplomatic importance. They were to travel by sea on HMS *Renown* and there was no question of their adored first-born leaving the comforts of home for such a length of time. Before and during the trip, the Duchess, especially, fretted at leaving her child behind: 'Feel very miserable at leaving the baby,' she wrote in her diary. 'Went up & played with her & she was so sweet.'

The Duchess knew that the child would be well cared for by the ever-vigilant Alla and by her grandparents, but she also knew she would miss so many stages of her baby's life, not least her first birthday. The King and Queen sent regular accounts of Elizabeth's progress, including how she waved goodbye, saying 'ta-ta' and 'by-eee'. Photographs of the tiny Princess were sent out, including one that showed a laughing baby; a note attached, written by the nanny, Clara Knight, read: 'If Mummy looks into my wide open mouth with a little magnifying glass, she will see my two teeth.'

When, at last, the royal parents arrived home their first thoughts were of their daughter, now a toddler. They moved with her to their new home, 145 Piccadilly, whose windows faced those of Buckingham Palace. When Elizabeth grew a little older she was given a small telescope which she could use to 'spy' on her grandfather the King who, in turn, would train his telescope from Buckingham Palace on her, so that they could wave at each other. It was not unknown for

King to visit his son and daughter-in-law and, with no thought for royal dignity, get down all fours so that Elizabeth could climb on his back for a ride around the room, something would not have dreamed of doing with his own children. When the toddler was two, he ame seriously ill and spent some time recuperating at Bognor Regis – with plenty of visits m his little granddaughter. Even stern Queen Mary unbent enough to enjoy time on the ch with her, making sandcastles.

Elizabeth's mother – brought up in a large family, enjoying country pursuits, games, outings I the support of several brothers and sisters – wanted to give her own child the same happy ldhood. Weekends were spent at Royal Lodge, Windsor, and soon the little girl received a sent that was to induce a lifelong passion: Peggy, a fat Shetland pony, was hers to love, look er and ride at Windsor. The Princess had already caught the family obsession with dogs but love of horses and the freedom they have brought her started in her very early childhood en Peggy, the first of many ponies, joined the royal household.

Below: Princess Elizabeth enjoys a ride on her tenth birthday in Windsor Great Park, accompanied by her riding master. The pony was a birthday present.

17

Princess Margaret

Although the month was August, the night was cold and the weather unseasonal. Thunder echoed and rolled around the hills, while frequent flashes of lightning lit up the sandstone walls and fairy-tale turrets of rain-lashed Glamis Castle, the ancient family seat of the Scottish earls of Strathmore and Kinghorne in the County of Angus.

Despite the pouring rain and the storm raging overhead, villagers, wrapped up against the elements, waited by the north gate of the castle for news of a royal birth – the first in direct line of succession to the throne in Scotland for more than 300 years. The Duchess of York, daughter-in-law to King George V and youngest daughter of the 14th Earl of Strathmore, had chosen to travel to her family home to give birth to her second baby. At 9.22pm on 21 August 1930, a 6lb 11oz girl, a second granddaughter to the King and herself fourth in line to the British throne, was born. Named Margaret Rose, she was said to be as pretty as a picture, with large blue eyes and a clear pink and white complexion.

Soon mother and baby travelled back to London to their home, just across Green Park from Buckingham Palace. As Margaret grew, she shared the same childhood delights and passions as her older sister 'Lilibet' (a family name coined by a very young Margaret, unable to pronounce 'Elizabeth'). They both enjoyed the countryside and riding, romping with their favourite corgis and picnicking outside, whether at Royal Lodge, Windsor, their weekend residence, or at Balmoral, the Royal Family's Scottish estate where the whole family then, as now, gathered for summer holidays.

While the children could gaze from their windows at the front of their home across to the grand palace where 'Grandpa England' lived with their grandmother, Queen Mary, their garden backed on to Hyde Park and many Londoners went out of their way to stroll past the railings to see the two little Princesses at play.

While Elizabeth had a serious, thoughtful streak, it was said that her little sister was full of fun and often mischievous. Family history records an occasion when the girls, accompanied by

Below: Glamis Castle, the Queen Mother's family home, where Princess Margaret was born in 1930.

Below right: Princess Margaret Rose, aged three, toddles in front of her nannies.

Above: Elizabeth and Margaret join their parents, now King George VI and Queen Elizabeth, on Buckingham Palace balcony on 12 May 1937, after the coronation.

their grandmother and mother, were taken to see the work of disabled ex-servicemen. The younger Princess spent some time examining a wheelchair, working out how to ring the bell – which she did with some vigour before anyone could stop her.

Despite their different natures, the two sisters were inseparable during early childhood. Both loved outdoor activities but while the quieter, less demonstrative Elizabeth was pony-mad, Margaret enjoyed play-acting and music, dancing and singing with noticeable ability from early childhood. Elizabeth observed her younger sister drawing all the attention and did not mind one bit. She is said to have remarked to her governess: 'It's so much easier when Margaret's there – everyone laughs at what Margaret says.'

They shared their nanny, Alla, and, as soon as they were old enough for lessons, were taught by their mother and their governess, Marion Crawford, who stayed with them for 16 years. Princess Margaret and her older sister were noted for their gentleness and beautiful manners; while their father took pleasure in his older child's intelligence and quiet self-possession, he doted on his younger daughter's joyful, outgoing nature. He described Elizabeth as 'my pride' while Margaret was always 'my joy'.

19

Prince Philip

When the young Princesses Elizabeth and Margaret began their history lessons, they knew little of their distant cousin Prince Philip of Greece, though, like the sisters, he was a great-great grandchild of the redoubtable Queen Victoria, who had died in 1901. However, the early childhood of the three young royals could not have been more different.

Elizabeth and Margaret, as the beloved grandchildren of the King of England, lived in comfort in a close and caring family. Their baby days and early childhood were ruled by the nursery routine dictated by their nanny and governess, which gave a sense of security.

Philip was born on 10 June 1921 at his parents' villa, 'Mon Repos', on the sunny island of Corfu. His soldier father, Prince Andrea (Andrew) of Greece, was commanding the Greek army's 12th division in Asia Minor and did not see his son for the first three months of his life.

Right: Prince Philip at the age of 14 months.

The young Prince came into the world during a time
[tu]rmoil in the Balkan nations. His mother, Princess
[Alic]e, and his four older sisters lived in the house left to
[the]m by his paternal grandfather, George I of Greece,
[wh]o had been assassinated in March 1913. Philip's uncle,
[Co]nstantine I, who ruled Greece during the first Balkan
[Wa]r, suffered exile as did his father, Andrea. Another
[unc]le, Alexander, who briefly took the Crown during
[Co]nstantine's exile, died of blood poisoning. His Russian
[rela]tions, the Romanovs – including his great aunts on his
[mo]ther's side, the Empress Alix and Princess Elisabeth,
[and] his father's cousin Tsar Nicholas II and his family –
[had] been murdered by Lenin's Red Army in 1918. Philip
[wa]s barely a year old when his father narrowly escaped
[bei]ng sentenced to death by the new Republican Greek
[gov]ernment. He and his family fled from their villa in
[Cor]fu into exile.

Although Prince Philip was, briefly, sixth
in line to the Greek throne, he has no
Greek blood. His great-grandfather was
King Christian IX of Denmark whose
son, Prince William, Philip's grandfather,
was sent to Greece at the tender age of 17
to be crowned their king. King George I
of Greece, as he became, had eight
children, one of whom, Andrea, was
Prince Philip's father.

Philip's mother, Alice, was Queen
Victoria's great-granddaughter. Her
mother, Princess Victoria, married
Prince Louis of Battenberg, who
eventually became First Sea Lord and
1st Marquis of Milford Haven. Alice,
despite being born deaf, was noted for
her beauty, poise and cleverness. Her
younger brother, Louis, became Admiral
of the Fleet, Earl Mountbatten of Burma.

Prince Philip's father met his mother
in 1902 when both were guests at the
coronation of King Edward VII, which
had been delayed because of the King's
sudden appendicitis. The young couple
fell in love and became engaged.

Above: Prince Andrea (Andrew) of Greece and Princess Alice
of Battenberg, Prince Philip's parents, married at Darmstadt,
near Frankfurt in Germany, in October 1903.

Andrea and Alice had married in 1903 after a short
engagement. The wedding, at Alice's family home,
Darmstadt, just south of Frankfurt, was a magnificent
affair, lasting two days. The couple lived in Athens where
they had four daughters, despite the often unsettling
political climate as the Balkan Wars put pressure on the
military and on the King and his family.

This pressure meant that the Greek royal family, including Andrea and Alice and their four daughters, were in exile in Switzerland in the months before Philip's birth in 1921. Suddenly the Greeks voted to restore the monarchy and they returned – Alice expecting her fifth and last baby. While Andrea, now a major-general in the Greek army, returned to his military duties in Athens, Alice and the children travelled across the sea to their villa on Corfu, where the family were helped by an English housekeeper, a handyman and Alice's elderly nanny, Miss Emily Roose. 'Mon Repos' had no modern comforts such as electricity or running hot water but it was secluded and in a beautiful position, looking over the Ionian Sea.

Contact with Andrea became difficult when, on 9 June, he was given command of a division leaving Athens for Smyrna, to lead troops in the on-going Turkish campaign. Early on the morning of the following day, Alice, now 36 years old, went into labour and was helped onto the villa's dining-room table by the local doctor who decided this was the best place for her to give birth. A baby boy, later registered as Philippos, was delivered at 10am. The child was sixth in line to the Greek throne.

Alice wrote to her family at Darmstadt that her new baby was 'a splendid healthy child'. She confirmed that she had had an easy delivery and was enjoying the pleasant sea-air from her chaise longue on the terrace. The blond-haired, blue-eyed Philip, the longed-for son, was the darling of a household full of women. He was a chubby, happy baby, fussed over by his adoring mother and four older sisters.

When Philip was three months old, Alice's father, Louis, Marquis of Milford Haven, died. She travelled with her infant son to Osborne House, on the Isle of Wight, for the burial. There the smiling baby was passed around an assortment of aunts and uncles for kisses and cuddles and general admiration. On their return to Corfu, Alice was surprised and delighted to find Andrea home on leave; he was thrilled to hold his baby son in his arms for the first time.

Right: Prince Philip, aged two, with his mother, Princess Alice, in 1924. The family were living in exile in a Paris suburb at this time.

Philip was almost a year old, and already standing up, when his maternal grandmother, the ~~newly~~ widowed Victoria, and Alice's sister, Louise, came to stay. The doting grandmother and ~~aunt~~ were delighted with the happy little boy. Louise wrote that he laughed all day and that she ~~had~~ never seen such a cheerful baby.

But not long afterwards the family had to flee for their lives. The Greek army was beaten in the ~~Tu~~rkish campaign, the country humiliated and Andrea's brother, King Constantine, abdicated ~~and~~ fled into exile. Philip's father was banished from Greece for life. The family slipped quietly out ~~of~~ Greece on the British cruiser *Calypso*. At the Corfu villa, Philip's sisters hastily packed essential ~~po~~ssessions, and burned letters, papers and documents before embarking for their new life in exile ~~Ph~~ilip, just 18 months old, remembered nothing of the escape, when he slept on board in a crib ~~ma~~de from a roughly converted fruit crate.

~~They~~ settled, eventually, in Paris where they lived at St Cloud, but by the time Philip was nine ~~his~~ mother had become ill and was taken to a Swiss psychiatric sanatorium. Philip had already ~~bee~~n sent to Cheam, an English preparatory school; his father moved to a small flat in Monte ~~Ca~~rlo; his sisters married and moved away. He chose a naval career, training at the Royal Naval ~~Co~~llege, Dartmouth, where, in July 1939, he was to meet his 13-year old cousin, Princess Elizabeth ~~a~~ meeting that was to change the course of his life.

Above: The eight-year-old Prince Philip (second left) has fun at an archery class at school in St Cloud.

Prince Charles

When Princess Elizabeth and Prince Philip made their first official overseas visit as a couple to France in the baking hot days of May 1948, no one guessed that the glamorous young woman who charmed the French public and dignitaries alike, might have been feeling unwell. The couple, married just six months earlier, were expecting their first child. But Elizabeth coped perfectly, keeping her happy news secret.

The Duke and Duchess of Edinburgh were still waiting for their first real home. Clarence House, next to St James's Palace in London, was being refurbished for them and they were living in a rented property, near Windsor. They moved back into Buckingham Palace, where the ornate Buhl Room was converted into a delivery suite for the arrival of the baby who would be second in line of succession to the throne. Royal babies were always born at home with top doctors and nurses in attendance. This tradition was broken only when Prince Charles' son, Prince William, was born in hospital – albeit in a private wing.

On the early evening of 14 November 1948, Philip – never the most patient of men – was dividing his time between swimming in the palace pool and playing squash with his equerry, Mike Parker. Elizabeth had gone into labour 24 hours earlier; she was attended by doctor Sir William Gilliatt and nursing sister Helen Rowe, so Philip knew she was in good hands and physical activity was the way he coped with the long, tense wait.

Suddenly King George VI's private secretary 'Tommy' Lascelles appeared at the door of the squash court. The news was good, and Philip raced upstairs, grabbing the roses, carnations and a bottle of champagne ordered earlier. As Elizabeth, sleepy from medication, opened her eyes, he handed her the flowers and kissed her as he gazed at their baby son, in a cot by her side.

Below left: Princess Elizabeth and her husband of six months, Prince Philip, on an official visit to Paris in May 1948, when she was expecting their first child.

Below right: Prince Charles, fair-haired and blue-eyed, was almost five months old when this photograph was taken at Buckingham Palace in April 1949.

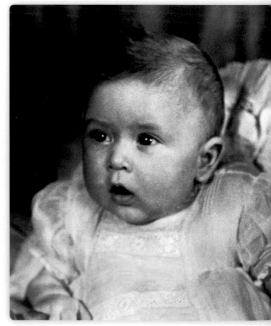

Her Royal Highness the Princess Elizabeth, Duchess of Edinburgh, was safely delivered of a ...nce at 9.14 o'clock this evening. Her Royal Highness and the infant Prince are both doing ...ll' read the handwritten notice attached to the Buckingham Palace railings by the King's ...ss secretary, raising a cheer and a rendition of 'For he's a jolly good fellow' from the 3,000 ...ople who had gathered outside, waiting for the news.

...By the evening of the following day, more than 4,000 telegrams had been received and the ...sents, from hand-knitted hats, bootees and matinee jackets to teddy bears, began to arrive. ...But although there were photographs of the baby and bulletins about him, one thing ...nained a mystery: what was he to be called? Speculation deepened as the name of the next ...r to the throne was not announced until his christening, a full month later.

...When the news came, on 15 December, that the baby was to be called Charles Philip Arthur ...orge, many were surprised. The name Charles had not been used by the Royal Family for ...ore than 300 years, after the unhappy reigns of Charles I and Charles II.

...Both Elizabeth and Philip enjoyed those early days of parenthood, when they were relatively ...e to spend time with their baby son. Prince Philip was a good and involved parent with all

Above: Proud parents: a delighted Princess Elizabeth and Prince Philip show off their first son, Prince Charles.

his children when they were little – playing with them, reading stories and teaching them to fish and enjoy outdoor pursuits.

The following year saw the family moving into Clarence House, refurbished at last. Charles was safely established in his blue and white nursery, sleeping in the cot that had belonged to his mother and aunt. The new nursery regime was overseen by nanny Helen Lightbody, an experienced Scottish nurse, whose strict manner gave her the nickname 'No Nonsense Lightbody', and a young girl who was to become an important part of Prince Charles' life: Mabel Anderson.

Mabel, a policeman's daughter, was 22 – almost the same age as the Duchess of Edinburgh – when she replied to an advertisement for an assistant nanny, not knowing it was from the royal household. Mabel was, said Charles, 'warm, loving, sympathetic and caring'. It was Mipsy, as her young charge called her, who put Charles to bed, read him stories, taught him to say his prayers and brush his teeth. It was she he turned to when he fell and grazed his knee or felt unhappy. Both he and, later, Princess Anne, clearly loved and listened to her and she has been invited to many private Royal Family gatherings over the years.

Right: Queen Elizabeth with her first grandson, Prince Charles, after his christening at Buckingham Palace in December 1948.

Below: Prince Charles, aged two-and-a-half, stands on the wall of Clarence House to wave to his parents as they pass by in a royal procession for the Festival of Britain. Charles and Prince Richard, the son of the Duke and Duchess of Gloucester, are in the care of nannies Ellen Woodburn (left) and Mabel Anderson.

Princess Anne

...precisely 3.30pm on 15 August 1950, a Royal Salute was fired in Hyde Park by the King's ...op of the Royal Horse Artillery. The gunfire welcomed the latest addition to the Royal ...ily, a baby girl, into the world. Prince Charles, almost two, was joined in the nursery by his ...er, who was born at home, Clarence House, just before noon, weighing exactly 6lbs. ...Her father, Prince Philip, brought bottles of champagne to toast her health with the staff, ...le her grandfather, King George VI, was tracked down on the grouse moors at Balmoral to ...old the good news. The new baby's grandmother, the Queen, visited twice that day to hold ...granddaughter.

...Two weeks later the baby's name was announced: Anne Elizabeth Alice Louise, Princess ...ne of Edinburgh. When the Registrar visited Clarence House to complete Princess Anne's ...h certificate, he handed Prince Philip his baby daughter's identity card, a ration book and ...tles of cod-liver oil and orange juice, as was the practice in those post-war years.

...The nursery routine accommodated the pretty blonde curly haired child. It soon became ...rious, however, that although the two children loved each other dearly and enjoyed playing ...ether, their natures were very different. Charles, thoughtful and shy, artistic and a sensitive ...dreamer, sometimes lacked confidence. His younger sister could be high-spirited and a little ...ighty. As soon as she could choose, this bright little tomboy preferred wearing dungarees or ...users to dresses.

...Anne loved sports and inherited her mother's passion for horses. She and brother ...arles learned to ride on a roan gelding called William and both became adept. Anne is ...orsewoman of the first order, eventually becoming a member of the British Olympic ...estrian team.

...But rosettes were in the future and Anne was a lively toddler of 18 months when her ...ndfather, the King, died in February 1952. Life changed in an instant. Charles and Anne, ...ldren of the new monarch, had to leave the familiar surroundings of Clarence House ...the overwhelmingly vast and grand Buckingham Palace, moving to the nursery floor ...ere familiar items from Clarence House – the large Tudor doll's house, toy soldiers ...d cuckoo clock – were waiting for ...m. It was here that they received their ...ly schooling from governess Catherine ...bles, their tutor and mentor until ...y started school.

Above: Baby Princess Anne, just one month old, cradled in the arms of her mother, Princess Elizabeth.

...ht: The different characters of ...ghing Princess Anne (aged two) ...d her more serious elder brother are ...tured in this photograph, taken ...Balmoral Castle, to mark Prince ...arles' fourth birthday.

Princes Andrew & Edward

Ten years after the birth of Princess Anne, the nation learned that The Queen was expecting another child. Prince Andrew Albert Christian Edward was born in the grand Belgian Suite on the ground floor of Buckingham Palace's garden wing on 19 February 1960. Soon after his birth The Queen wrote to her second cousin, Lady Mary Cambridge: 'The baby is adorable, an is very good, and putting on weight well. Both the older children are completely riveted by him and all in all, he's going to be terribly spoilt by all of us, I'm sure.'

Four years later, on 10 March 1964, Prince Edward Antony Richard Louis was born in the same room, completing the family. The two boys, Andrew and Edward, were the first children to be born to a reigning monarch since their great-great-great grandmother, Queen Victoria, gave birth to her youngest daughter, Beatrice, in 1857. Andrew, and later Edward, were looked after by the favourite royal nanny, Mabel Anderson, with the help of a newly appointed assistant, the 29-year-old June Waller.

Following royal tradition, Andrew was taught at home by a governess (and by The Queen who helped him learn to read and count) until he was eight, when he went away to school, as did his younger brother.

It seems Andrew was a mischievous young boy, being caught tying together the shoelaces of castle guards as they stood at attention – and somehow turning the swimming pool at Windsor Castle into a giant bubble bath on one memorable occasion.

Buckingham Palace's Belgian Suite, named for Queen Victoria's favourite uncle, King Leopold of Belgium, was converted into a delivery ward for the arrival of The Queen's two younger sons. But now the grand three-roomed apartment is where visiting heads of state stay, when they visit the British Royal Family.

Andrew enjoyed several outings with his nursemaid, June, who wrote to a friend in March 1963: '... I took Andrew on a *bus*!! to Paddington Station to see the trains. He was thrilled to bits and couldn't see everything fast enough – we even bought sweets in a kiosk there and no one gave us a second glance, it was marvellous.' She wrote of another outing: 'We also went to

Left: Prince Andrew at seven months holds hands with his sister, Princess Anne, and his father, the Duke of Edinburgh.

Left: The Royal Family at Frogmore, Windsor: Prince Andrew, aged five, rocks his baby brother, Prince Edward, watched by The Queen, Prince Philip, Prince Charles and Princess Anne.

Below: The Queen's two younger sons, the Princes Andrew and Edward, romp in the grounds of Buckingham Palace in March 1966.

zoo about a fortnight ago – two other children and nans. It was
t fun – again, no one recognized him – but then again we looked
er a disreputable lot in mackintoshes, etc! He muddled in with
he other children at the chimps' tea party and he might have
onged to anyone!'
n another letter, June described the eight-month-old Edward,
ing him an 'absolute poppet' and a 'funny, cheeky little
g – not a bit like Andrew'. At that age Edward, the proud
sessor of four teeth, and weighing 20lb 8oz, enjoyed
pelling himself across the floor on his elbows, knees and
my. 'London being what it is, the colour of his clothes
obody's business,' wrote June, adding that
young Prince 'looks permanently like
ruffy, cheeky little London sparrow,
ept when he is clean in bed.'
Both Andrew and Edward went
he exclusive Heatherdown Preparatory
ool near Ascot, in Berkshire, before
owing in their older brother and father's
tsteps to the rugged Gordonstoun school
Moray, Scotland.

Royal Grannies & Nannies

Below left: Princess Elizabeth, aged five, and a friend enjoy a walk in the park with nannies Margaret Macdonald and, pushing baby Princess Margaret's pram, Clara Knight.

Below right: Princess Elizabeth with her grandmother, Queen Mary, and grandfather, King George V, arrives for a service at Westminster Abbey in July 1934.

On Prince Charles' 60th birthday in November 2008, an exhibition illustrating his early life was displayed at Windsor Castle. Among the photographs on show were those of an expertly crafted green stoneware mug, with a Celtic-style initial 'M' incised in the oxidized glaze. The words 'Charles' and 'Gordonstoun' appear on the base. This treasured object was made in the school pottery studio by the 17-year-old Charles in 1965, not for a family member, but for his former nanny, Mabel Anderson, who had been a central figure for the boy as he grew up.

Royal parents have heavy demands on them and, however much they want to be 'hands-on', it has never been possible to spend as much time in the nursery as they might like. They rely on grandparents for help, but royal children have the additional support of nannies, nursery staff and sometimes a governess, all of whom tread the fine line of giving loving care to their charges, without taking the place of the royal mother or father.

Royal sisters the Princesses Elizabeth and Margaret were dearly cherished by their grandparents, King George V and Queen Mary, whose own children were not nearly as indulged as their granddaughters. They were also loved and looked after by their nanny, Clara Knight ('Alla'), once their own mother's nanny, and, later, when Elizabeth was four, by 'Bobo', Margaret MacDonald, who became a lifelong companion, taking on the task of royal dresser when Elizabeth became Queen. Their friendship ended only when Bobo, then 89, died in 1993; hers is understood to be one of the few funerals ever attended by Her Majesty.

Another stalwart is Mabel Anderson ('Mipsy'), who came to care for baby Charles and, later, Princess Anne. Mipsy has become a beloved friend, accompanying the family on holiday treats and spending time with The Queen and Prince Charles, who described her as 'a haven of security, the great haven'. Mabel, when retired, returned to royal service

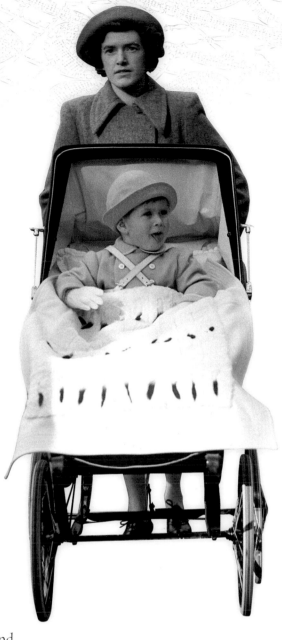

ve: In this charming photograph, Princess
beth holds the baby Princess Anne after
christening while two grandmothers, Queen
beth (later the Queen Mother) and the
wed Queen Mary, look after Prince Charles.
ce Philip stands in the background.

Right: Nanny Mabel
Anderson takes Prince
Charles for an outing to
St James's Park, London,
on his second birthday in
November 1950.

porarily, to help Princess Anne care for her son, Peter. Mabel was
a grace and favour home in an apartment at Frogmore House in
dsor Home Park.

ing George VI, The Queen's father, died when Charles and Anne were
young, but Queen Elizabeth the Queen Mother loved young children and
close to both of them. Charles, especially, felt comfortable with his grandmother and
ed to her with his worries and problems.

When Prince William, son of Prince Charles and Princess Diana, was born, his mother
lved to give her children constant attention and affection. Just a few weeks after his birth,
and Charles were committed to a long tour of Australia. Diana refused to leave her baby
ind. There was worldwide approval when pictures were shown of William in the arms of
nanny, Barbara Barnes, being carried from the aircraft onto Australian soil.

arbara Barnes was William's first nanny but she was succeeded by Olga Powell who was
William and his younger brother, Harry, for 15 years until their mother died in 1997. Up
il Olga's death in 2012, they kept in touch, writing to her regularly – and she was invited to
liam's wedding in 2011. Olga saw the boys through their parents' divorce but it was their
nd and last nanny, Alexandra 'Tiggy' Legge-Bourke, who helped them through the dark
s following their mother's untimely death.

Both William and Harry rely on their grandmother, The Queen, for advice and support.
en William went to Eton in 1995, he was delighted that the school was within walking
ance of Windsor Castle – where he could join his grandmother for Sunday tea.

Above: Olga Powell was
nanny to the Princes
William and Harry.

Right: Born to be King: on 15 December 1948, Prince Charles sleeps in his mother's arms after his christening as his grandparents, King George VI and Queen Elizabeth, and father, Prince Philip, watch fondly. The baby is dressed in the Royal Family's traditional Honiton lace christening gown.

Royal Nurseries

Royal babies have traditionally spent their formative years in the sensible surroundings of a room or suite of rooms known as 'the nursery', a domain ruled over by a nanny or nannies, more often than not helped by a nursery nurse and other assistants.

Queen Victoria and Prince Albert created a charming nursery at Osborne House on the Isle of Wight for their children, where they could enjoy family time away from public view. The nursery, with its child-size dining table and chairs, remains today as it was in 1870.

Princess Elizabeth's first nursery was small, a room in the family's temporary residence at Bruton Street, furnished and decorated by her maternal grandmother, Lady Strathmore. But soon there was much more space for the infant Elizabeth and, later, her sister Margaret Rose, when the family moved to 145 Piccadilly, a London mansion where a suite of rooms on the top floor were converted to accommodate a day nursery, a night nursery and a bathroom. The rooms all opened on to a landing, with large windows overlooking Green Park. A sense of security and comfort was established with a regular routine, nursery meals and the ever-present nanny – in the small Princesses' case, the reassuring figure

Above: An invoice dated July 1845 for toys supplied to the royal nursery for Queen Victoria's children.

Right: The nursery at Osborne House on the Isle of Wight, with some toys belonging to the children of Queen Victoria.

lla. There was a rocking horse and other toys, but
re were also baby garments hung to dry on airing rails.
ile the children played or sat to eat their breakfast
unch, nanny would sit in her rocking chair, knitting
mending clothes. After bathtime in the evening, she
uld tell the girls stories before bedtime.

From early days the children were taught good
nners and restraint – when Princess Elizabeth began
rawl, she was allowed only one toy at a time to play
h. During summer holidays with their mother's
ents at Glamis Castle, the children stayed in the
ient nursery wing that had seen their aunts and
les grow up.

Both Prince Charles and Princess Anne were cocooned
he nursery wing at Clarence House for the first years
heir lives. The day nursery, with its chintz-covered
nchairs, its fireplace, radiogram and desk, was like a
ng-room in a comfortable home, but there were also
all tables and chairs, designed with young children in
nd. The children were both still under the age of five
en their grandfather died, their mother became Queen
d they moved to Buckingham Palace, where everything
s on a larger scale. By the time Charles was five, part of
day nursery at the palace was converted into a school
m, complete with a desk and blackboards, so that his
ucation could begin at home with his new governess,
therine Peebles.

It was in the Buckingham Palace nursery that the
dler Charles played with some of his best-loved toys,
luding wooden bricks packed into a trolley bearing the
rds 'Prince Charles Express', but it was at Windsor
stle that he enjoyed one of his favourite games: taking
green Sunbeam Coupe pedal car from the nursery and
ing it up and down the Grand Corridor.

Prince Charles' own sons, William and then Harry,
re brought up in their top-floor nursery at Kensington
ace, under the watchful eye of their much-loved
nny, Olga Powell. Mrs Powell, who worked at
nsington Palace for 15 years, had her own small bedsit
rtment, next door to the boys' rooms, so that she
uld keep an eye on them at all times.

Above and below: The night and day nurseries at 145 Piccadilly,
the home of the Princesses Elizabeth and Margaret.

Above: Catherine Peebles, the governess who taught Prince
Charles in the converted nursery at Buckingham Palace.

Prince William

Right from the start, Prince Charles and Princess Diana were determined that their children should have as normal a childhood as possible, although they were aware that they would be unable to spirit them away from the spotlight of public interest that would be a focus from the moment of birth.

Prince William's debut was different from that of earlier royal births. He was born in an ordinary hospital, albeit in a private wing, the first 'heir presumptive' (an heir, other than the first, in line to the throne) not to make his entrance in one of the royal residences. This was seen by many as a sign that the young Prince was entering a changing world, far different from that occupied by his father in 1948.

Crowds of well-wishers and journalists were waiting early on the morning of 23 June 1982 to see 33-year-old Prince Charles, heir to the throne, standing proudly outside St Mary's Hospital, Paddington, tenderly holding his newborn son, who would also one day be king. The then unnamed baby, the tag still on his wrist identifying him only as 'Baby Wales', slept

Below: Prince William's first Christmas: with his parents at Kensington Palace in 1982.

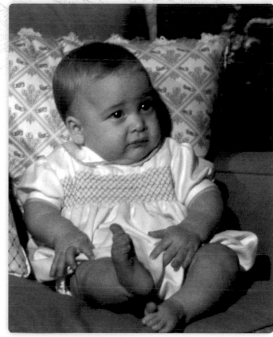

Above left: Before she had children of her own, Lady Diana Spencer (later the Princess of Wales) loved looking after the children when she worked as a nursery school assistant.

Above: Six-month-old William sits propped against cushions at Kensington Palace.

Left: Prince William entertains and steals the show at his brother Harry's christening in December 1984.

...cefully in his father's arms, while cameras flashed and journalists and television crews ...outed questions to the new parents. 'The birth of our son has given us both more pleasure ...an you can imagine,' said a tired and delighted Prince. 'It has made me incredibly proud and ...mewhat amazed.'

...Prince William Arthur Philip Louis of Wales had entered the world at 9.03pm on 21 June ...the private Lindo Wing of the hospital. He was driven to Kensington Palace, his home for ...e next 16 years.

...William's mother, Princess Diana, nicknamed her baby 'Wills' and, later, 'Wombat', two ...mes that have stayed with him. Diana, who had worked as a nursery assistant and as a

nanny, loved young children and was a devoted and imaginative mother, keeping her vow to be closely involved with her children's care. She often defied royal convention in William's upbringing, choosing his first name and buying his clothes herself. Although she had a full schedule of duties she tried to negotiate these around William's timetable.

Diana was demonstrative with her children and William was picked up, cuddled and kissed often in public. Prince William saw far more of his parents than royal babies in the past and, when it was time for him to start learning, there was no governess – he was to go to nursery school like other small children. His mother chose a small private establishment in Notting Hill and, as often as she could, accompanied her three-year-old son to school and collected him herself. She was keen that he should learn to interact with other children and to understand that there was a world outside the palace.

Some might say the much-loved William was, perhaps, a little too indulged by his doting mother and, by the time he found his feet at nursery school, was inclined to want to rule the roost and have things his own way. For a while the tabloid press nicknamed the little boy 'William the Terrible' for his sometimes public tantrums. A new nanny, the no-nonsense Ruth Wallace, joined the nursery floor at Kensington Palace to help her colleague, Olga Powell; the two nannies, given authority by Charles and Diana to discipline the spirited youngster, soon reminded him of the value of good manners and taught the young Prince how to behave on all occasions.

When William was four-and-a-half he started attending the upmarket Wetherby Pre-Preparatory School at Notting Hill, less than a mile from his home in Kensington Palace, and found himself kept busy. In sharp contrast to the two days a week at nursery school, he was now having to be up by 7.30 each weekday morning, washed and dressed before eating breakfast and being taken to his new school where he started lessons in earnest. Reading and writing, the first steps in maths, singing lessons and competitive sport were all on the timetable. After-school activities included piano and swimming lessons, often with Diana. Those formative years with loving parents and caring nannies have stood William in good stead for his later life.

Right: Watched by his cousin Laura Fellowes, a mischievous Prince William, aged three, is caught on camera during the wedding of Prince Andrew and Sarah Ferguson at Westminster Abbey in 1986.

Far right: The shape of things to come: William, watched by Prince Andrew, tries out the controls of his uncle's helicopter on board HMS *Brazen* in 1986.

LT HRH PRINCE ANDREW

Prince Harry

[Wil]liam's younger brother, Henry Charles David Albert, was born on [15] September 1984, again at St Mary's Hospital, Paddington. The new baby, [kn]own affectionately as 'Harry', was calm and placid and, in his first few years, [wa]s a quieter child than his big brother, William. Very soon the boys became [play]mates and good friends.

Their two down-to-earth nannies, Ruth Wallace and Olga Powell, gave the [you]ngsters a steady routine. William and Harry were, in Olga's words, 'just like [any] other children'. 'Their upbringing was very normal and their parents wanted [the]m to have as ordinary a childhood as they could,' she told journalists. 'If they [saw] a muddy puddle they wanted to jump in it and if there was something to [clim]b, they wanted to climb it.'

Despite hours apart whilst William was at school, there was still time for the [two] brothers to play together, donning their Supermen outfits or army gear for a [gam]e of soldiers, and time for fun at weekends when life went at a more leisurely [pac]e. Whenever possible the family travelled to Highgrove, their country home in [Glo]ucestershire, where both boys enjoyed helping their father, Prince Charles, in [the] garden, or on the river where they would learn the rudiments of fishing. There [wa]s farmland to explore, fields to run round and the boys' pony, Smokey, would [be] saddled up for early riding lessons.

Prince Harry, just two-and-a-quarter years younger than William, was [cat]ching up fast, following his brother from nursery and pre-prep schools. In 1992 [he] joined William at Ludgrove School in Berkshire, where they were both pupils [un]til William left for Eton in September 1995, followed by Harry in 1998.

Life for both boys was varied – their mother, wanting them to experience [ord]inary life, took them to theme parks, burger restaurants and even to night [she]lters for the homeless so that they could understand other people's lives. [So]mething they both enjoyed were visits, with Diana, to rugby matches. [Pri]ncess Diana was the unofficial mascot of the Welsh rugby team and [too]k her sons to international games at Cardiff's Millennium Stadium. They [res]ponded by joining in the singing of the Welsh National anthem – having [lea]rned the words in Welsh.

Being royal could not protect the Princes from the divorce of their parents in [19]96, nor from the tragic death of their mother in a car accident the following [ye]ar, when Harry was not yet 13, and William 15.

Peter & Zara Phillips

Below: Three generations: Princess Anne holds her firstborn, Peter Phillips, after his christening at Buckingham Palace. The Queen is clearly taken with her first grandchild.

The Queen's eldest grandchild made history when he was born during the middle of the morning on 15 November 1977. His mother, Princess Anne, was driven to St Mary's Hospital, Paddington, by her then husband, Captain Mark Phillips, in the early hours of that day. When the baby boy arrived, weighing 7lb 9oz, a 41-gun salute, the usual signal of a royal birth, was fired at the Tower of London, but the baby, whose names were not yet announced, was given no title. He was born plain Master Phillips because Princess Anne, in spite of being The Queen's daughter, possesses no hereditary title; her son became the first royal baby to be born a commoner for more than 500 years.

But that did not put a damper on the rejoicing in his paternal grandparents' village of Great Somerford in Wiltshire, where a peal of bells was rung at the church of St Peter and St Paul in celebration of the new arrival.

The Queen was among the first of a clutch of visitors at the private wing of the hospital and she was clearly delighted with her first grandson, whose name, Peter Mark Andrew Phillips, was later announced.

Above: Peter Phillips enjoys his father's company at the Badminton Horse Trials in 1983.

When Peter eventually arrived home to Gatcombe Park in Gloucestershire, it was to the welcoming arms of his mother's nanny, Mabel Anderson, who had been persuaded to come out of retirement to look after the latest royal baby. Miss Anderson, much loved by all the Royal Family, stayed with young Peter until he went to the prep department of Beaudesert Park School, Minchinhampton, within walking distance of Gatcombe, just before a baby sister was born on 15 May 1981.

Zara Anne Elizabeth and Peter grew up together with the freedom to enjoy country life. Gatcombe is situated in beautiful unspoiled countryside and they were born into a family whose main interest was horses. They had access to the stables of their parents, both expert riders, and ponies of their own, which they learned to master almost as soon as they could walk – and Zara ultimately followed in Princess Anne's footsteps by competing in the Olympics.

If there was sadness at the departure of nanny Mabel Anderson, returning to a well-earned retirement, there was also fun to be had with their new nanny, Pat Moss, who would take them out, often over to their paternal grandparents' farmhouse, just 15 miles away.

Zara followed her brother to Beaudesert School and Port Regis preparatory School in Dorset. In line with royal tradition, the siblings studied at Gordonstoun in Scotland, where they both excelled in sports and where Peter, who was chosen to be head boy, played rugby for the school, while Zara represented it at hockey, athletics and gymnastics.

Above: Two-year-old Zara Phillips rides on the shoulders of her mother, Princess Anne.

Zara's unusual name was the inspiration of her uncle, Prince Charles. 'The baby made a rather sudden and positive arrival,' recalled Princess Anne, 'and my brother thought Zara (a Greek name meaning "bright as the dawn") was an appropriate name.'

Below: Zara and Peter Phillips and their cousin, Prince William (centre), share a joke on Buckingham Palace balcony during their grandmother's birthday parade in 1984.

The birth of the first child of Prince Andrew and Sarah Ferguson, the Duke and Duchess of York, was eagerly anticipated in August 1988. The baby would be The Queen's fifth grandchild and the royal mother-of-four showed her own impatience about the baby's arrival; during a royal visit, asked when it was due, she said: 'These wretched babies don't come until they're ready. They don't come to order.'

A clue that the birth was imminent was the return home, from Singapore where he was serving as a Royal Navy pilot, of Prince Andrew, who drove his wife to London's Portland Hospital on the morning of 8 August. He went with her to her room on the third floor and was beside her during a short labour. The baby girl, unnamed for some days, but dubbed 'Baby Yorklet' by her fond parents, was born in the early evening, weighing 6lb 12oz. 'The baby is very pretty,' Andrew told reporters, 'But then I am very biased.'

By the time he arrived at the end of the week to pick up his wife and his red-haired daughter, fifth in line to the throne, those waiting outside the hospital had enjoyed witnessing the arrival of Princess Diana and her two sons, the new baby's first cousins, William and Harry (the latter mischievously sticking his tongue out at photographers) and other royal visitors. On leaving hospital, Sarah wore a teddy-bear shaped badge stating 'I'm a mum'. The family of three, in their blue Jaguar, drove to a waiting aircraft that delivered them safely to Scotland, where they were to stay with The Queen at Balmoral and ask her approval for the new baby's name.

Below left: The Duke and Duchess of York with Princess Beatrice, just two weeks old.

Below right: Beatrice holds tightly to her mother's hand as she arrives for her first day at Upton House School, Windsor, in 1991.

The child was christened Princess Beatrice Elizabeth Mary at the Chapel Royal, St James's Palace, on 20 December.

A new nanny, Alison Wardley, was engaged to look after Beatrice, who moved with her parents back to the family home, the seven-bedroomed Castlewood House in Surrey, where they were living until the much larger Sunninghill Park mansion in Windsor Great Park was completed. In fact the new 12-bedroomed house was still not ready by the time the Duchess went into labour with her second child, less than two years later.

The birth of Princess Eugenie, on 23 March 1990, proved difficult as the unborn child was in a breech position, necessitating an unexpected Caesarean section. But when the Duchess of York checked out of the Portland Hospital a week later, the 7lb 1oz infant was already named Eugenie Victoria Helena, after Queen Victoria's favourite granddaughter, Victoria Eugenie.

Nanny Alison Wardley now had her hands full with the two little girls, but she and they had a new home to move to just six months after Eugenie's birth. Sunninghill Park, with its cinema, swimming pool, tennis courts and children's nursery, was at last ready. Beatrice, now two, had a bedroom painted pink and lemon, while baby Eugenie's night nursery was a pretty lemon and blue.

The Yorks broke with royal tradition when it was Eugenie's turn to be christened. She was baptized in public during a regular Sunday morning service at St Mary Magdalene Church at Sandringham on 23 December, two days before Christmas Day, 1990.

Above left: The Duchess of York gives her daughter Eugenie a fond kiss after the baby's christening at Sandringham Church in December 1990. Cousins Zara Phillips (bottom left) and Prince Harry (right) join the christening party. Princess Beatrice can just be seen at the bottom of the photograph.

Above right: Princesses Beatrice and Eugenie enjoy a game of football at a charity polo match in September 1991.

Lady Louise Windsor & James, Viscount Severn

Prince Edward's daughter's entry into the world was both dramatic and traumatic. Lady Louise Windsor, born after her mother, Sophie, Countess of Wessex, had previously suffered an ectopic pregnancy, arrived four weeks early. The Countess was rushed to Frimley Park Hospital in Surrey on 8 November 2003 and had to undergo an emergency Caesarean operation, during which her life was endangered by blood loss. Little Louise, weighing just 4lb 9oz at birth, was taken immediately to the specialist neo-natal unit at St George's Hospital in south London as a precautionary measure, where she stayed for five days, before being sent back to Frimley Park.

Her father, Prince Edward, Earl of Wessex, The Queen's youngest son, was away on royal duty, on a state visit to Mauritius, when his daughter was born, but he flew back immediately to be with his wife and baby. Once it was known that both mother and baby were out of danger, the Countess, who clearly intended to be a hands-on mother, spent as much time with her new daughter as possible, friends reporting that the infant, whose full name is Louise Alice Elizabeth Mary Mountbatten-Windsor, was a 'real cutie-pie' and 'a perfect jolly little baby'.

Louise began to thrive and was discharged from hospital on 23 November, four days after her mother. In December she was taken to join the rest of the Royal Family for the traditional Christmas celebrations at Sandringham in Norfolk. It soon became evident that she was doted on not only by her parents, but also by her paternal grandmother, The Queen, who spent more time than usual fussing over the latest addition to the family.

The birth in 2007 of Louise's brother, James Alexander Philip Theo Mountbatten-Windsor, also at Frimley Park Hospital, was far less difficult. Prince Edward was with his wife in a private suite at the hospital as his son was delivered, by Caesarean section, by royal gynaecologist Maurice Setchell on 17 December. The Prince, clearly relieved, told well-wishers and journalists outside the hospital that his baby son was 'small, cute and cuddly'. He added that the baby's arrival was 'a lot calmer than last time, I'm glad to say'.

Below left: Prince Edward, Earl of Wessex, carries his toddler daughter, Lady Louise Windsor, on to dry land after a Royal Family boating holiday in the Hebrides in 2006.

Below right: Sophie, Countess of Wessex, smiles as she and her husband, Prince Edward, leave hospital with their baby son, James, Viscount Severn.

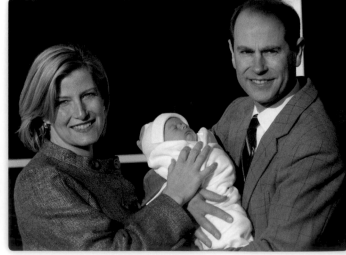

Left: Enjoying a family day out: Prince Edward and his children at the Royal Windsor Horse Show in 2010.

The Earl and Countess of Wessex live at Bagshot Park, near Windsor Castle, where their children – known to be close and fond of each other – often go to see their grandmother, who likes to spend time with them. Like their grandmother, Louise and James are both passionate about horses and keep their ponies stabled in the Royal Mews at the castle, often riding out with the Queen. Although their grandmother wears her traditional headscarf, she insists that the children wear hard hats.

The Earl and Countess of Wessex are protective of their children and try to keep them out of the limelight, especially Louise who was born with a rare eye condition, exotropia, that affects her sight. Despite this she is an avid reader, and is keen on ballet as well as riding.

Like their cousins Peter and Zara Phillips, neither Louise nor James has taken the title of Prince or Princess as is usual for grandchildren of a reigning monarch. As the daughter of an Earl, Louise becomes 'Lady' while James is known by one of his father's titles, Viscount Severn.

Savannah & Isla Phillips

The Queen's first great-grandchild, born on 29 December 2010 to her eldest grandson, Peter Phillips, and his Canadian-born wife, Autumn, made history when it was disclosed that the baby, who was 12th in line to the throne at the time of her birth, had dual Canadian and British citizenship. The child, whose name was as yet undisclosed, became the first Canadian in the British line of succession.

The public was not kept in the dark for long over the name of Princess Anne's first grandchild. At a church service on 2 January at The Queen's Sandringham estate in Norfolk, attended by the Royal Family, the Rector of Sandringham, the Reverend Jonathan Riviere, made mention in a prayer for 'Peter and Autumn Phillips and their daughter Savannah'. Although the name caused a few eyebrows to be raised in Britain, Canadians and Americans accepted it without comment. It has no special meaning other than its usual description of an open plain in the landscape, but the name is now in common use across the Atlantic, where it is increasingly popular.

Savannah's father – at the request of his parents, and because Princess Anne holds no hereditary title – has no royal title, and his daughter follows suit.

Peter Phillips met Autumn Kelly in 2003 at the Montreal Grand Prix, where they were both working – he in sports sponsorship and she as a management consultant. They became engaged in 2007 and were married at St George's Chapel, Windsor, in May the following year. Autumn Phillips, a former Roman Catholic, was accepted into the Church of England shortly before their wedding, because the 1701 Act of Settlement decrees that her husband would have had to give up his right to the throne had she not done so.

Below: Aunt Zara Phillips keeps an eye on her niece Savannah, while Savannah's parents, Peter and Autumn Phillips, look after their younger daughter, Isla. Zara, The Queen's oldest granddaughter, married to rugby star Mike Tindall, announced in summer 2013 that she was expecting her first baby in early 2014.

Above: Time for a bottle: Isla Phillips, during horse trials at Gatcombe Park in September 2012.

The first year or so of their marriage was spent in Hong Kong, where Peter Phillips worked the sports sponsorship division of the Royal Bank of Scotland. They moved back to London on before Savannah Anne Kathleen, weighing 8lb 8oz, was born at the Gloucestershire oyal Hospital near Gatcombe Park, the home of her grandmother, Princess Anne. Her father as present throughout the birth. The Queen, who said she was 'delighted' at the arrival of e latest addition to the Royal Family, became the first reigning monarch to have a great-andchild since Queen Victoria more than 100 years before.

Savannah's first public outing was at Gatcombe Park when the annual horse trials were held ere in March 2011, when the baby was almost three months old. She was christened at Holy oss Church, Avening, Gloucestershire, the following month.

Soon afterwards, in October 2011, Peter and Autumn announced they were expecting other child and the more conventionally named Isla Elizabeth Phillips, weighing 7lb 4oz, as born in the same hospital as her older sister on 29 March 2012. It was thought to be no incidence that her second name was the same as that of her great-grandmother who was lebrating her Diamond Jubilee that year.

Isla was christened at St Nicholas' Church, Cherington, Gloucestershire, on 1 July that year.

Royal Babies of the Past

Some eyebrows were raised when Princess Anne and, later, Prince Charles and Princess Diana, broke with royal tradition by choosing to have their babies delivered in hospital. Royal babies have nearly always been born at home, in a palace. But in Tudor times strict rules and ritual applied to royal ladies about to give birth. The 'confinement' of a queen was literally that: she was sent into seclusion in a suite of rooms which included a Great Chamber, a birthing chamber and an oratory with a font, so that an ailing newborn could receive immediate baptism.

Anne Boleyn, pregnant with what royal astrologers confidently predicted was her husband King Henry VIII's longed-for male heir, took to her chamber on 26 August 1533. Before her formal entrance she had attended Mass and invited members of the Court to a banquet in her Great Chamber. Afterwards, all male members of the court, the household, and even the King himself, were excluded from these rooms, the women within taking over traditional male duties such as pantry men and butlers. Anne, escorted by high-born ladies, was taken to her bedchamber, which, following the rules laid down, was oppressively dark and stuffy. Tapestries showing the story of St Ursula covered walls, the ceiling and even the windows. A thick carpet was laid and keyholes and any aperture that let in the tiniest glow of light were covered. The great bed, with a wool-stuffed mattress, fine linen sheets and large pillows filled with downy feathers, was ready for her. Alongside it were two cradles: one the formal state cradle, upholstered in red and gold, and with a crimson and ermine counterpane to match that on the

Right: Greenwich Palace, named Palace of Placentia ('Pleasant Place') by King Henry VIII who was born there in 1491. His daughter Elizabeth, later Queen Elizabeth I, was also born there, in 1533. The palace was demolished in 1694.

A View of the ANCIENT ROYAL PALACE, call'd, PLACENTIA, in East Greenwich.
Copied from an Engraving published by the Society of Antiquaries of London.

Left: King Henry VIII with his son, Edward, and his daughters, Mary Tudor and Elizabeth. The figure seen in the background is their jester, Will Sommers.

Below: A portrait of the young Princess Elizabeth (later Queen Elizabeth I) by Robert Peake the Elder in 1603.

ueen's bed; and another 'cradle of tree' made of carved ood, painted gold. Braziers had been lit and open bottles scent perfumed the air, making the room hot and airless.

The rules for the birth of a royal child dictated that the nfinement should begin four to six weeks before the pected date of delivery. Anne, probably pregnant before r wedding on 25 January 1533, went into labour on September, giving birth to a healthy baby girl. The official ry was that the baby was premature.

That baby, who was welcomed by her father despite longing for a son, eventually became the long-reigning ueen Elizabeth I. She was, of course, known as the irgin Queen' (although that status has been questioned some historians) and bore no children so never had to e the claustrophobia of the royal bedchamber.

The protocol for royal birth had been exercised for nturies but these 'rules' for the confinement, followed Anne Boleyn and other queens and royal ladies, were fined by another royal mother in 1485. Lady Margaret aufort, married at the age of 12 to Edmund Tudor in ovember 1455, was only 13 when he died just a year er. She was pregnant and gave birth to her son, Henry, Pembroke Castle on 28 January 1457. Henry was later defeat Richard III at the Battle of Bosworth Field on August 1485, becoming Henry VII, the first Tudor King England. Lady Margaret, who promoted and founded ucational establishments (including St John's College, mbridge, founded by her estate), detailed in writing the nditions that should be followed for all royal births.

In 1688 a son was born to the Catholic King James II and his second wife, Mary of Modena. British people had tolerated James' Catholic government because he had no heir to perpetuate it. But when Mary's pregnancy was announced, there was consternation and rumours spread that the Queen was not pregnant, but pretending to be so and that another woman's baby would be smuggled into the birthchamber. So Mary had to endure giving birth with a room full of witnesses – accounts vary between 76 and 200. Despite this invasion of the mother's privacy rumours persisted that the baby was not hers but was brought by sleight-of-hand into her bed by means of a warming pan. Thus began the tradition, that most royal mothers could not avoid, of the birth being verified by a minister of the Crown. This custom, to prove legitimacy, was observed until well into the 20th century, although the minister has waited in an adjoining room. When she was expecting the future Edward VII in 1841, Queen Victoria decided that only one Cabinet minister would be required, and from then on the Home Secretary was asked to attend. The last occasion when the Home Secretary was called upon to carry out this delicate duty was at the birth of Princess Alexandra of Kent in 1936.

Royal children of the past have often been brought up separated for long periods from their parents. Political situations might mean exile, while the very real fear of plague in the cities gave rise to the setting up of households in the country where the children were sent with their wet-nurses and a bevy of servants to look after them. In charge was a high-born lady or governess who would oversee the household. 'Rockers' were employed to keep the royal cradle on the move, while the wet-nurse, preferably one who was healthy looking and rosy cheeked, was an important member of the household. She was important enough to the baby's well-being to have another servant taste her food – just in case someone tried to slip in poison that would affect her royal charge. These separate households were expensive to maintain with their yeomen, grooms, a chaplain, a clerk, minstrels and flute players, acrobats, a laundress and wood-bearers, among others.

Left: A miniature showing the young Princess Victoria with her mother, Louise, Duchess of Kent.

Below: Princess Victoria, later Queen Victoria; an 1830 portrait in oils by Richard Westall.

Royal children born in later centuries had a safer, if much more dull, time. Queen Victoria's mother, the overbearing Marie Louise Victoria, Duchess of Kent, employed a food-taster just in case her daughter was threatened. A child of the early 19th century, Princess Victoria was brought up in the family apartments at Kensington Palace, forbidden to mix with other children and with little chance of seeing much of the outside world. She was in turn spoiled and punished by her mother and governess. When she was good she was allowed to ride her white donkey in Kensington Gardens, led by a groom using the ribbons. With her hair in its carefully constructed corkscrew curls she would eat breakfast, attended by her page, on the palace lawns in summer.

But she was under constant surveillance from over-protective adults – never allowed alone in a room with a servant (unless a governess or nurse), never allowed to walk downstairs without holding someone's hand and always sleeping in the same room as her mother. When she had a tantrum – and she often did – she was locked in her room as a punishment.

Right: A painting by Sir Edwin Landseer of Queen Victoria and Prince Albert's eldest child, the Princess Royal, Victoria, born in 1840. Shown with the baby is Prince Albert's favourite greyhound, Eos.

The sad deaths of two royal babies left the way clear for Queen Victoria, later known as 'the grandmother of Europe', to become Queen in 1837. Although she was the granddaughter of King George III, her three uncles and her father, Prince Edward, Duke of Kent, all came before her in the royal line. Her two eldest uncles, the Prince Regent (later King George IV) and the Duke of York, had no children; her other uncle, the Duke of Clarence, not only managed to produce ten illegitimate children with actress Dorothea Jordan, but also, later, two baby girls with his wife, one born in 1819, the same year as Victoria. But both the infants, who took precedence over Victoria in the line of succession, died soon after birth. Victoria was less than a year old when her father and her grandfather, the King, died in 1820. Her uncle, the Prince Regent, became King George IV, and the next brother, the Duke of York, died in 1827. The Duke of Clarence inherited the throne, as King William IV in 1830 and, on his death in 1837, Victoria, just 18, became Queen.

Her marriage to her cousin, Prince Albert, was a love match and they went on, famously, to have nine children. The eldest, also named Victoria, was born on 21 November 1840. It is said that Queen Victoria did not enjoy pregnancy, thought breastfeeding a disgusting practice and viewed newborn babies as ugly little creatures. However, she enjoyed their antics as toddlers and spent a lot of time at her much-loved Osborne House on the Isle of Wight, sketching them as they played. But as they grew and developed individual personalities, she found them hard to understand and cope with. Especially difficult, to her mind, was the behaviour of her oldest son and heir, Albert (Bertie) Edward. His personality matched her own and she dealt with the sulks and fits of temper which so upset her by keeping him on a very tight rein – as her mother had with her.

When Bertie, Prince of Wales, eventually succeeded in 1901, he was almost 60 and had been married to the outgoing Princess Alexandra of Denmark for 38 years. Alexandra loved her babies – and dreaded Queen Victoria's interference in their upbringing. Each of her six children

Left: An elderly Queen Victoria in 1896, photographed with her great-grandson, Prince Edward, who became, briefly, King Edward VIII, before his abdication in 1936. Edward is dressed in traditional clothes of the day for small boys.

Below: Prince Edward (later King Edward VII) and Princess Alexandra with four of their children. The future King George V (who was to become Queen Elizabeth II's grandfather) stands next to his father.

.s, apparently, born prematurely. This frustrated her other-in-law who wanted to be present and give advice their births. One biographer suggests that the canny exandra deliberately gave Victoria the wrong delivery tes, so that she could avoid the unwelcome presence in birthing chamber.

Alexandra was the first royal mother to show what we uld regard today as modern care for her children. She s devoted to each of them and loved to race up to their rsery, donning an apron, to bathe them herself and, th goodnight kisses, tuck them up in bed. She was able give so much of herself to their care because by the time husband became King they were grown-up, and the ungest, Alexander, and the oldest, Albert, already, sadly, ad. Her second son, George, became King George V, ndfather to Queen Elizabeth II, in 1910.

Royal Christenings

Above: A precious silk and lace 16th-century christening robe, thought to have been made for Princess Elizabeth (later Queen Elizabeth I) in 1533.

Soon after the birth of Princess Elizabeth in 1926, the chairman of the National Jewellers' Association arrived at the family home in Bruton Street. He carried an exquisitely wrapped present for the baby, made by members of his organization. The beautiful silver porringer, a little bowl with ivory handles carved to resemble thistles and a cover decorated with an ivory and silver coronet, would, he hoped, be placed 'upon the breakfast table of the first baby in the land'.

The baby received other silver gifts from her godparents (or 'sponsors' as royal godparents are known) at her christening in the private chapel at Buckingham Palace at the end of May. Although the ceremony was a family occasion, there were present ten 'Children of the Chapel Royal', choirboys with unbroken voices who wore crimson and gold uniform with old-lace jabots, bringing colour and traditional music to the ceremony. The service was conducted by the then Archbishop of York, Cosmo Lang.

The little Princess was carried into the chapel in the arms of her nanny, Clara Knight. It was she who came to the rescue when the sobbing baby, dressed in the fine Honiton lace and silk christening robe worn by royal babies since the days of Queen Victoria, refused to be comforted, as the family gathered around the ornate font. Alla, who had come prepared, dosed her tiny charge with several spoonfuls of traditional old-fashioned dill water.

The small party of close family and friends made their way back to Bruton Street for a celebratory tea party, the centrepiece of which was an elegant cake, decorated with the white roses of York surrounding a small silver cradle, and cut by the Duchess of York.

Elizabeth's sister, Princess Margaret Rose, was also christened at Buckingham Palace by Archbishop Cosmo Lang, and the venue for the ceremony, on 30 September 1930, was the palace chapel. Margaret's

Royal christenings of the past invariably featured the traditional family Honiton lace christening robe and the beautiful silver-gilt Lily Font, commissioned by Queen Victoria in 1840 and first used for the christening of her daughter, Victoria, in 1841. The water used to baptize the baby is sent from the river Jordan. The ceremony, which lasts about 30 minutes, is conducted by an archbishop, often the Archbishop of Canterbury. The Royal Family, godparents and guests stand near the font, waiting for the baby to be carried into the room by his or her nanny, accompanied by a lady-in-waiting. After the christening ceremony and the singing of hymns or anthems, the baptismal register is signed, before a reception where lunch or tea, depending on the time of day, is served, along with christening cake.

...ove: The sun streams into St George's Chapel, Windsor, in
...s painting by Sir George Hayter of the christening of Queen
...toria's eldest son, Albert Edward, later King Edward VII.
...e Royal Family's silver-gilt Lily Font is clearly shown.

...ht: Four generations of monarchs: Queen Victoria holds
... baby who would be King Edward VIII, on his christening
..., 16 July 1894. The baby, dressed in the beautiful Honiton
... christening gown first worn by his great-grandmother, is
...ked on either side by his grandfather (later Edward VII) and
...her (later George V).

...ristening cake, made in Scotland, was so large that there
...s enough to send each household in the village of Glamis,
...ar her mother's family home, a slice.
...Gifts, whether to celebrate the birth or the christening,
...e showered upon royal babies. In the year following
...zabeth's birth, her parents, the Duke and Duchess of
...rk, embarked, without her, on a six-month tour of
...stralia. When they returned it was with three tons of
...s – including several parrots – for their baby daughter.

Right: Born to be King: Prince William was christened at Buckingham Palace on 4 August 1982. This christening photograph shows members of the Royal Family and William's godparents: Sir Laurens Van der Post, Princess Alexandra, Duchess of Westminster, ex-King Constantine of Greece, Lady Susan Hussey and Lord Romsey.

Three of the children of The Queen and Prince Philip were baptized in the Buckingham Palace Music Room, an imposing chamber with a high-domed ceiling, arched windows and columns painted deep blue to look like lapis lazuli. Prince Charles, Princess Anne and Prince Andrew, all wearing the family christening gown, were welcomed to the fellowship of the Church, surrounded by their godparents, or sponsors.

Prince Edward was the exception, being christened in the private Chapel at Windsor Castle on 2 May 1964 by the then Dean of Windsor, Robert Woods. Charles and Andrew were christened by the Archbishop of Canterbury, Dr Geoffrey Fisher, while Dr Cyril Garbett, Archbishop of York, officiated at Princess Anne's baptism. Prince Andrew's nurse, June Walle reported that her young charge behaved very well at his baptism – not crying 'except for two little squeaks'.

The fabulous silver-gilt Lily Font is kept, with other royal treasures, in the Tower of London, except when it is brought to Buckingham Palace or Windsor Castle for a christening ceremony.

Above: The glorious Lily Font made in 1840–41 and used for royal christenings.

Left: Detail of the decoration on Prince Charles' official christening cake, 1948.

Princes William and Harry were both christened by then Archbishop of Canterbury, Robert Runcie, but, while William's ceremony took place, as had his father's, in the Buckingham Palace Music Room, Harry was baptized in St George's Chapel, Windsor.

Christening cakes for royal babies are always splendid confections but the little Prince Charles, christened in December 1948, had not one, but three, all on display during the family reception in the White Drawing Room at Buckingham Palace, after the religious ceremony. The first was a redecorated version of the top tier of his parents' wedding cake, made glorious with intricate 'lace' icing topped with a baby doll dressed in a magnificent robe,

The precious Honiton lace gown had been worn by royal babies at their christenings for 167 years and was beginning to look a little tired when The Queen decided to commission a hand-made replica from royal dressmaker Angela Kelly. The beautiful copy of the original gown was ready in time for the baptism, in April 2008, of baby James, Viscount Severn, the infant son of the Duke and Duchess of Wessex.

Below: Prince Edward, Earl of Wessex, and Sophie, Countess of Wessex, with their son, James, Viscount Severn, at his christening. The baby is wearing the christening gown newly commissioned for the April 2008 event by his grandmother, The Queen.

sewn by members of the Royal School of Art Needlework, sleeping in a silver cradle. The second was an enormous coronet-topped, three-foot (one-metre) high cake, made by students from the National School of Bakery with ingredients contributed from countries of the British Empire. The third cake, of two tiers, given by the Universal Bakery and Food Association, was decorated with silver ornaments made by disabled silversmiths.

Prince William's cake was also a redecorated version of the top tier of his parents' wedding cake. As with most royal babies, he was allowed to be star of the ceremony. But nursery routine is all-powerful and, once the champagne and cake were brought out and the reception began, William was whisked away to the nursery by his nanny.

All The Queen's children and grandchildren had splendid christening presents, one of the most magnificent being the antique silver-gilt cup, given to Prince Charles in 1948 by his great-grandmother and godparent, Queen Mary. The beautiful object was made by English silversmith Thomas Heming in 1773 for King George III, who had given it as a christening gift to the son of a friend.

Royal Succession

Succession to the throne in the 21st century is not such a contentious issue as in the days when battles were fought to claim the Crown and reigning monarchs were killed or had to flee into exile.

In 1066 William, Duke of Normandy, seized his chance when Edward the Confessor died with no heir. William, emerging victorious over Harold Godwinson, who had reigned for just a few months, established a dynasty that ended in civil war as rival factions supported two claimants to the throne: Stephen (who reigned until 1154) and Matilda, daughter of Henry I. Matilda's son, Henry II, eventually succeeded, the first in a long line of Plantagenets whose rule ended with the death of Richard III, defeated at the Battle of Bosworth in 1485 by Henry Tudor, who became King Henry VII.

Richard allegedly destroyed potential Plantagenet successors by killing Henry VI, his own brother, George, and his two young nephews – the uncrowned Edward V and his brother, Richard, Duke of York – who disappeared in suspicious circumstances.

Fears over the succession were raised again with the death of the childless 'Virgin Queen', Elizabeth I. The Crown went to James VI of Scotland, son of Mary, Queen of Scots, who had been executed in 1587 on Elizabeth's orders. James became James I of England and was succeeded by his son Charles, who upset Parliament so much that civil war erupted and all thought of succession ceased as Charles was executed in 1649, and the monarchy suspended. But the interregnum ended with the recall from exile of the dead King's son, Charles II, in 1661.

Below: The reigning monarch: Her Majesty Queen Elizabeth II.

Above: Prince Charles, the Prince of Wales and Duke of Cornwall, is first in line to the throne.

he next upset was in 1685 when Charles II died, to be succeeded by his brother, James II,
ose Catholic policies impelled his overthrow in favour of his (Protestant) daughter Mary
her husband William of Orange, who ruled jointly from 1689 until Mary's death in 1694,
n William ruled alone until he died in 1702. He was succeeded by his sister-in-law, Anne.
her death the throne went to her second cousin, George of Hanover, a deeply unpopular
who spoke not a word of English.
he succession ran more or less smoothly until the abdication of Edward VIII in 1936,
n The Queen's father became King. With the accession of Queen Elizabeth II in 1952
succession became secure. She is the mother of four children, grandmother to eight and a
t-grandmother. In 2013, laws changed to allow equal succession rights to boys and girls –
uring that William and Catherine's eldest child is third in line to the British throne.
s we celebrate the arrival of the latest addition to the Royal Family, our nation is assured
the monarchy is secured for another generation.

It was the forced 'abdication' of James II in 1688, leading to the invitation to his daughter Mary and
her husband William, rather than James' young son, to rule that led to the 1689 Bill of Rights and
the 1701 Act of Settlement, determining the basis for the succession, not only by descent, but also by
Parliamentary statue. These acts established that the Sovereign rules through Parliament, which can
regulate the succession to the throne. If the Sovereign is deemed to have misgoverned (as in the case
of James II) he or she may be deprived of the title.

Changes were made to rules for the succession in 2013. The previous acts specifically excluded
Roman Catholics from the throne and banned the marriage of a sovereign to a Roman Catholic.
Now the spouse of a reigning monarch may be a Roman Catholic. The new Succession to the Crown
Act 2013 also decrees that females born in the line of succession will have exactly the same rights as
males. An older sister will not now have to step aside in favour of her younger brother, although this
change will not apply retrospectively to the current line of succession.

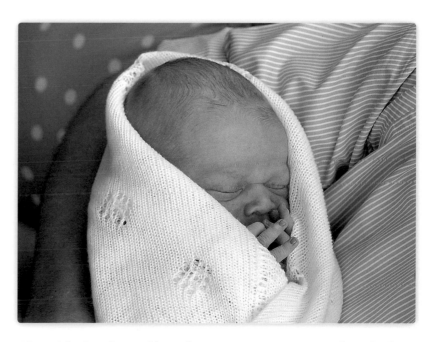

ove: Prince William, Duke of Cambridge, will
day succeed his father, Prince Charles.

Above: Third in the royal line of succession: Prince George of Cambridge.

61

The House of Windsor

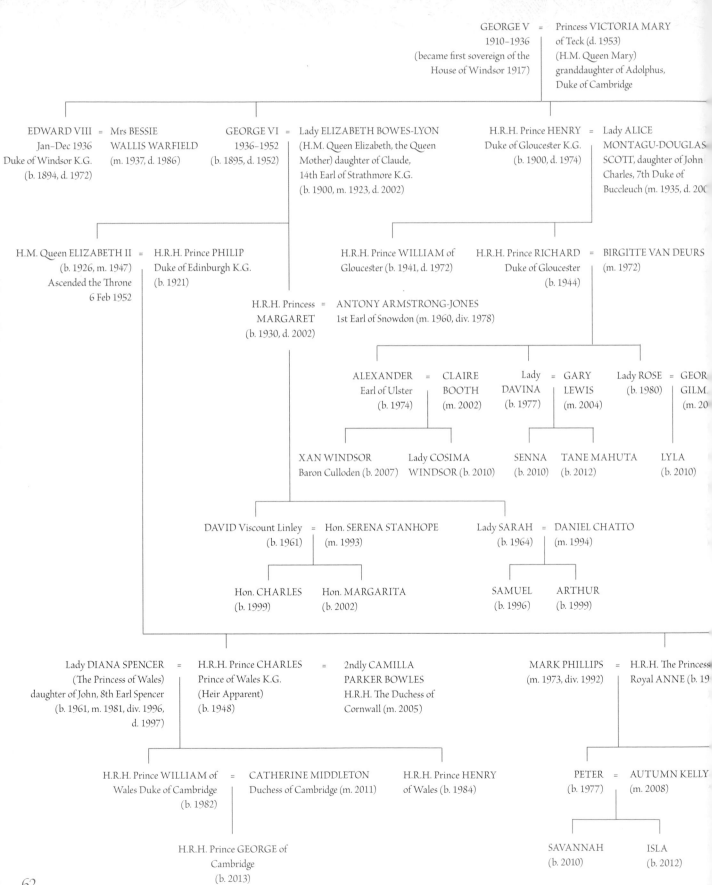

GEORGE V = Princess VICTORIA MARY
1910–1936 of Teck (d. 1953)
(became first sovereign of the (H.M. Queen Mary)
House of Windsor 1917) granddaughter of Adolphus,
Duke of Cambridge

EDWARD VIII = Mrs BESSIE
Jan–Dec 1936 WALLIS WARFIELD
Duke of Windsor K.G. (m. 1937, d. 1986)
(b. 1894, d. 1972)

GEORGE VI = Lady ELIZABETH BOWES-LYON
1936–1952 (H.M. Queen Elizabeth, the Queen
(b. 1895, d. 1952) Mother) daughter of Claude,
14th Earl of Strathmore K.G.
(b. 1900, m. 1923, d. 2002)

H.R.H. Prince HENRY = Lady ALICE
Duke of Gloucester K.G. MONTAGU-DOUGLAS
(b. 1900, d. 1974) SCOTT, daughter of John
Charles, 7th Duke of
Buccleuch (m. 1935, d. 200

H.M. Queen ELIZABETH II = H.R.H. Prince PHILIP
(b. 1926, m. 1947) Duke of Edinburgh K.G.
Ascended the Throne (b. 1921)
6 Feb 1952

H.R.H. Prince WILLIAM of
Gloucester (b. 1941, d. 1972)

H.R.H. Prince RICHARD = BIRGITTE VAN DEURS
Duke of Gloucester (m. 1972)
(b. 1944)

H.R.H. Princess = ANTONY ARMSTRONG-JONES
MARGARET 1st Earl of Snowdon (m. 1960, div. 1978)
(b. 1930, d. 2002)

ALEXANDER = CLAIRE
Earl of Ulster BOOTH
(b. 1974) (m. 2002)

Lady = GARY
DAVINA LEWIS
(b. 1977) (m. 2004)

Lady ROSE = GEOR
(b. 1980) GILM.
(m. 20

XAN WINDSOR Lady COSIMA
Baron Culloden (b. 2007) WINDSOR (b. 2010)

SENNA TANE MAHUTA
(b. 2010) (b. 2012)

LYLA
(b. 2010)

DAVID Viscount Linley = Hon. SERENA STANHOPE
(b. 1961) (m. 1993)

Lady SARAH = DANIEL CHATTO
(b. 1964) (m. 1994)

Hon. CHARLES Hon. MARGARITA
(b. 1999) (b. 2002)

SAMUEL ARTHUR
(b. 1996) (b. 1999)

Lady DIANA SPENCER =
(The Princess of Wales)
daughter of John, 8th Earl Spencer
(b. 1961, m. 1981, div. 1996,
d. 1997)

H.R.H. Prince CHARLES =
Prince of Wales K.G.
(Heir Apparent)
(b. 1948)

2ndly CAMILLA
PARKER BOWLES
H.R.H. The Duchess of
Cornwall (m. 2005)

MARK PHILLIPS = H.R.H. The Princess
(m. 1973, div. 1992) Royal ANNE (b. 19

H.R.H. Prince WILLIAM of =
Wales Duke of Cambridge
(b. 1982)

CATHERINE MIDDLETON
Duchess of Cambridge (m. 2011)

H.R.H. Prince HENRY
of Wales (b. 1984)

PETER = AUTUMN KELLY
(b. 1977) (m. 2008)

H.R.H. Prince GEORGE of
Cambridge
(b. 2013)

SAVANNAH ISLA
(b. 2010) (b. 2012)

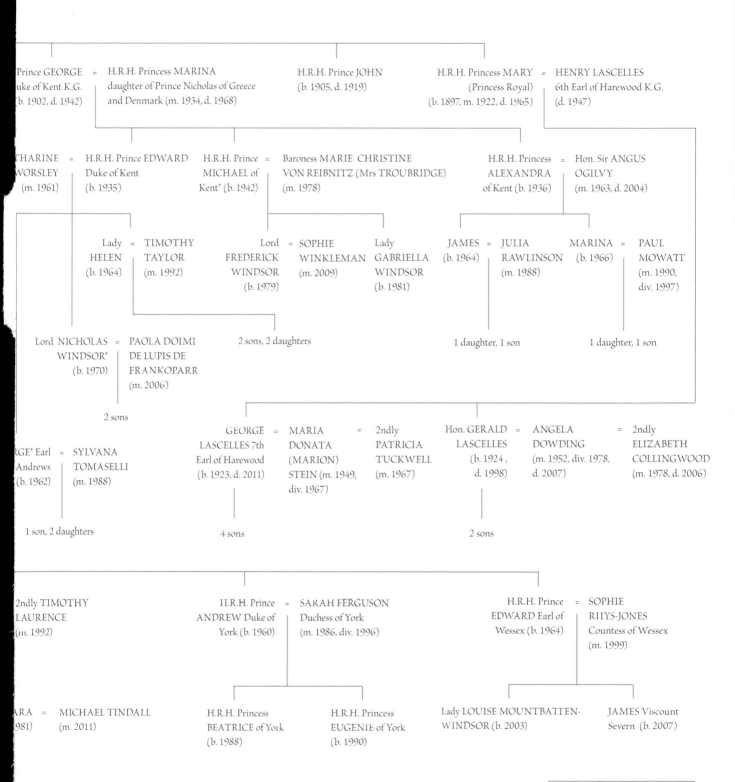

Prince GEORGE = H.R.H. Princess MARINA   H.R.H. Prince JOHN   H.R.H. Princess MARY = HENRY LASCELLES
Duke of Kent K.G.   daughter of Prince Nicholas of Greece   (b. 1905, d. 1919)   (Princess Royal)   6th Earl of Harewood K.G.
(b. 1902, d. 1942)   and Denmark (m. 1934, d. 1968)   (b. 1897, m. 1922, d. 1965)   (d. 1947)

CATHARINE = H.R.H. Prince EDWARD   H.R.H. Prince = Baroness MARIE CHRISTINE   H.R.H. Princess = Hon. Sir ANGUS
WORSLEY   Duke of Kent   MICHAEL of   VON REIBNITZ (Mrs TROUBRIDGE)   ALEXANDRA   OGILVY
(m. 1961)   (b. 1935)   Kent* (b. 1942)   (m. 1978)   of Kent (b. 1936)   (m. 1963, d. 2004)

Lady = TIMOTHY   Lord = SOPHIE   Lady   JAMES = JULIA   MARINA = PAUL
HELEN   TAYLOR   FREDERICK   WINKLEMAN   GABRIELLA   (b. 1964)   RAWLINSON   (b. 1966)   MOWATT
(b. 1964)   (m. 1992)   WINDSOR   (m. 2009)   WINDSOR   (m. 1988)   (m. 1990,
                              (b. 1979)   (b. 1981)   div. 1997)

Lord NICHOLAS = PAOLA DOIMI   2 sons, 2 daughters   1 daughter, 1 son   1 daughter, 1 son
WINDSOR*   DE LUPIS DE
(b. 1970)   FRANKOPARR
          (m. 2006)

2 sons   GEORGE = MARIA   = 2ndly   Hon. GERALD = ANGELA   = 2ndly
                    LASCELLES 7th   DONATA   PATRICIA   LASCELLES   DOWDING   ELIZABETH
GE* Earl = SYLVANA   Earl of Harewood   (MARION)   TUCKWELL   (b. 1924,   (m. 1952, div. 1978,   COLLINGWOOD
Andrews   TOMASELLI   (b. 1923, d. 2011)   STEIN (m. 1949,   (m. 1967)   d. 1998)   d. 2007)   (m. 1978, d. 2006)
(b. 1962)   (m. 1988)   div. 1967)

1 son, 2 daughters   4 sons   2 sons

2ndly TIMOTHY   H.R.H. Prince = SARAH FERGUSON   H.R.H. Prince = SOPHIE
LAURENCE   ANDREW Duke of   Duchess of York   EDWARD Earl of   RHYS-JONES
(m. 1992)   York (b. 1960)   (m. 1986, div. 1996)   Wessex (b. 1964)   Countess of Wessex
                                                          (m. 1999)

ARA = MICHAEL TINDALL   H.R.H. Princess   H.R.H. Princess   Lady LOUISE MOUNTBATTEN-   JAMES Viscount
1981)   (m. 2011)   BEATRICE of York   EUGENIE of York   WINDSOR (b. 2003)   Severn (b. 2007)
                    (b. 1988)   (b. 1990)

* Not in succession to the throne

63

The Order of Succession

1. HRH Prince Charles, The Prince of Wales
2. HRH Prince William of Wales, The Duke of Cambridge
3. HRH Prince George of Cambridge
4. HRH Prince Henry of Wales
5. HRH Prince Andrew, The Duke of York
6. HRH Princess Beatrice of York
7. HRH Princess Eugenie of York
8. HRH Prince Edward, The Earl of Wessex
9. Lady Louise Windsor
10. James, Viscount Severn
11. HRH Princess Anne, The Princess Royal
12. Peter Phillips
13. Savannah Phillips
14. Isla Phillips
15. Zara Tindall (Phillips)
16. David Armstrong-Jones, Viscount Linley
17. The Hon. Charles Armstrong-Jones
18. The Hon. Margarita Armstrong-Jones
19. Lady Sarah Chatto
20. Samuel Chatto
21. Arthur Chatto
22. HRH Prince Richard, The Duke of Gloucester
23. Alexander Windsor, Earl of Ulster
24. Xan Windsor, Baron Culloden
25. Lady Cosima Windsor
26. Lady Davina Lewis
27. Tane Mahuta Lewis
28. Senna Lewis
29. Lady Rose Gilman
30. Lyla Gilman